No Turning Back

No Turning Back

Jacqueline Allen

Superior Publishing LLC.

CONTENTS

DEDICATION viii

Introduction 1

1 | It's Not the End 3

2 | Stop Running Looking Backwards 6

3 | No Turning Back 9

4 | The Painful Truth 12

5 | Love Broke 15

6 | A Wake Up Call 18

7 | The Past 21

8 | Going Forward 24

9 | Me and My Big Mouth 28

10 | Speak Over Your Life 30

CONTENTS

11 | A Better Me   33

12 | The Fight of My Life   35

GIVING THANKS TO GOD   38

Copyright © 2024 by Jacqueline Allen

All rights reserved. No part of this book may be reproduced in any manner whatsoever without written permission except in the case of brief quotations embodied in critical articles and reviews.

Superior Publishing LLC. 2024

Thanking God for allowing me the ability to write 3 books.
Lord I give YOU all the glory!
All three books were inspired by my life and how God is always with me,
leading me and guiding me through each and every thing that has happened in my life.
Book Titles:
Through the Pain
Starting Over
No Turning Back

Introduction

This book, No Turning Back, is to encourage someone that there is nothing wrong with moving forward. We serve a God who is faithful and loves us. He has brought us through the pain, and allowed us to start over.

A lot of times, we try to take matters into our own hands, and make an even bigger mess out of things. But we serve a God that take our mess and turn it into a message. But we've got to surrender it all to Him and trust Him to work it out. There are things that we will hold in our hearts, that will keep us from moving forward. Be very careful because the heart will lie to you.

Jeremiah 17:9 The heart is deceitful above all things and desperately wicked. Who can know it? God knows our hearts.
Proverbs 4:23 Tells us to guard our hearts above all else, because everything we do flows from it.

We serve a God that knows everything about us. And He has made it possible for us to move forward. He will turn our pain into a praise and our mess into a message. So everyone will know that He can and will do the impossible.
He has already brought us through so much and allowed us to start over, and to do that, we must surrender everything.
Let His will be your will. Let His thoughts become your thoughts. Let His peace become your peace. A peace that passes all understanding.

In order to move forward, we have to stop running back to the past.
Proverbs 3:5-7, says, Trust in the lord with all our heart and lean not on our own understanding. 6. In all our ways we get to acknowledge him and he will direct our path. 7. Be not wise in your own eyes, Fear the lower and he shall direct your path.

There are going to be a lots of roadblocks set before you. There's going to be lots of family members, friends and foes that are going to walk out on you. Let them go and pray for them and continue to move forward leading the way for them to also surrender their life to God.

The road moving forward is going to be very lonely. But I always remember God sees, God cares, and God will provide.

It takes more energy to give up than it does to keep moving forward. So keep going. Keep moving with your eyes straight ahead. You are a victorious! You are a conqueror! Take the step forward and don't turn back.

1

It's Not the End

It is the beginning of a new life, and a new you! Because you've decided to move on with your life, there are so many things trying to hold you back. Now it's time to let them go because you cannot move into your future while living in your past.

What's done is done and what's gone is gone. One of the best lessons we can learn in this life is to let go and move on.

It's okay to look back, but don't let your past keep you from moving forward. Sometimes our lives will be completely shaken, changed, and rearranged to relocate us in the place we are meant to be. We can't live our lives to please others. It is God who we need to please. Never underestimate the power in you to be a difference and to make a difference in this world.

It is important to learn to be done with certain situations without feeling mad or bothered. Instead, move on and be at peace with yourself. One day, you will look back, and realize that you had to go through stuff, in order to shape you for what you were getting ready to face moving on.

Your heart will heal Psalms, 34:18;
your season will change Ecclesiastes 1:22;

your tears will dry Revelations, 21:4

So rest knowing that God is in control and the storm will end. God is restoring your life and everything the devil has stolen from you. In this season of your life, I don't know how God is going to do it and I don't know when He's going to fix it, but I do know that He's going to do it, and make away for you. Be the best you can be and know that God is with you always.

Moving forward makes you a winner! When you were in your dark place, you probably thought you were being buried and wanted to give up, but you were actually being planted. And now you are growing in new water and new sunshine.
I love it when God interrupts my thoughts and reminds me that this battle is not mine but it is His.
In this new beginning, stop talking negatively to yourself. Your thoughts feed your faith and it also feeds your fears. If you can change the way you think you will change the way you live.
Tell yourself:
Deuteronomy 28:13 I am blessed
Lamentations 3:24 God is your portion
Psalm 73:26 God is your strength
Psalm 142:5 God is your refuge
Psalm 26:3 God walks with you
After all you have been through, you are still standing, so it's time for your new beginning.

Father, I am thanking you in advance for what you are about to do in our life. Lord thank You for the new things that are manifesting in our lives now.

Remember the struggles are not to destroy you but to strengthen you to keep moving. Please don't ever give up on God or yourself. Your faith can move mountains Matthew 17:20. God said He will supply all your needs, so you'll have all you need for your new start in life.

2

Stop Running Looking Backwards

A lot of us are trying to run just like Jonah 1:17. God already knew that we were going to run. Jonah ran because of disobedience. I ran because of shame, guilt, and pride. So just as God provided a huge fish for Jonah. We also get swallowed up in the fish with trials, and pains that we face in life. But God is showing us that when He gets ready for us there's no where we can run. There's no where we can hide from Him. We try to run from ourselves and God. When God gets ready for us, there's no running, and no hiding, only crying out and praying to God to deliver us out of the belly of the big fish of life.

God hears our prayers and he shows us what He wants from us. We have to be obedient, loving and gentle whether we want to be or not. If we just surrender and let God be God and work things out for us, there will be no need to run looking backwards. We serve a God that is faithful to deliver us at any time. We need Him, but we have to be like Shadrach, Meshach and Abendnego in Daniel 3.

We have to make up our minds that we will not bow to the problems, situations and circumstances that are brought before us. Even if we fall in the fires of life, it cannot overtake us, and it can't consume us, because we are not alone.

Jesus is faithful to His word to always be right there with us. But there's something we have to be willing to do. We have to have a heart like Job. A heart for God, to believe that God can and He will. We have to have an attitude like Job. In the word, Job 13:15, says, "Though he slay me, yet still I will trust in Him."

Things will come against us, but God has equipped us with everything we need to move forward and not run looking backwards.

The way we move forward is to trust in the Lord with all of our heart and lean not on our own understanding. Move forward with a renewed mind and a renewed heart.

God is putting us in a position where we are the head and not because of anything we have done to deserve it. But He's preparing a table for us in the presence of our enemies. And our cup is running over and over because He loves us that much. God wants us to love others the same way. We can pray for them, but we can't accept what God has for them. We can only try to lead them to it.

We have to run and faint not. I fail many of times during this race, but God. I was able to get back up and run on a little further. Along the way, I got tired and the weight from the tiredness started to weigh me down but God. That tiredness, started dropping off, piece by piece, and I was able to run a little further. I started feeling the strength of an eagle. Some might not know about the strength of an eagle. So here's a definition; for centuries, people have seen eagles as a symbol of beauty, bravery, courage, honor, pride, determination, and grace. This bird is important and symbolic to humanity because of his characteristics. God put a lot of love and care in an eagle, because He wanted to give us the strength of the eagle. Isaiah 40:31, says,"But those who hope in the Lord will renew their strength. They will soar on wings like eagles. They will run and not grow weary. They will walk and not faint." That's the strength God blessed me with and He will bless you too. It is the strength we need to get us to where He's trying to take us. I've done lots of crying along the way but I know God was with me. Psalms 56:8 says, "You keep track of all my sorrows.You have collected all my tears in your bottle and recorded it."

All of my tears are in His book and I feel like God took the tears that were meant to destroy me and use them to save me. God promised me that I would reach my goal if I faint not. I will keep running forward because there is no turning back.

3

No Turning Back

In this life, there will be many trials and tribulations along the way, that we will have to face. But we can take comfort in the fact, that we have a loving Father that cares for us. We need to know that no matter what, we can find shelter in His arms. We have nothing to fear. We are loved and cherished by a kind and loving God. A God that redeemed us from who we used to be. He has brought us through the pain, and has allowed us to start over again. So why would we want to go back to where we once were?

God will keep us from all danger if we allow Him. Isaiah 26:3, says "You will keep in perfect peace, those whose minds are steadfast because they trust in God."

One day while praying and talking with the Lord, I said,

"Lord I have let a lot of wasted years pass me by." And He said to me,

"Those years were not wasted. Those were the greatest years of your life.Because you were spending time with me.Getting to know me and I was preparing you for the things I wanted you to do. So the next few years will be even greater and I will get the glory."

I want to encourage someone to enjoy where you are while you are waiting to move forward. James1:22 tells us that we must be doers of the word, and not just hearers only. If we just follow God after He deliver us, We will see the deliverance that God will bring on the day that you decide to move forward.

When things come against you, God will command you to stand firm and it will be good for you. Just to listen to the Master's voice. God will help us to put on a cheerful courage and even in our worst times rejoice in His love and faithfulness.

God has commanded us to go from strength to strength, so we can stand firm and move on when He wants us. After this neither death nor hell will be able to turn us around. When you have to stand firm, it's the time that you will use to renew your mind and renew your strength for some greater advances in due time.

We have to be an immovable rock and stand firm with Jesus no matter what. When things come against us, we are to be ready for action, expecting further orders, and waiting patiently for God's voice to say, "Go forward!"

Proverbs 3:5 says, "Trust in the Lord with all your heart and lean not on your own understanding, but acknowledge Him and He will direct thy path.

Isaiah 45:2 says, "When we acknowledge God, He will go before us and make our crooked places straight."

It is time to move forward. The only way to move forward is to give God total and complete control over every area of our life.

Once we do that we can start seeing the works God has started.

Stay positive because a positive mind will find opportunity in everything.

4

The Painful Truth

People don't hurt us, we hurt ourselves. We bring things on ourselves. We block our own blessings, and we let ourselves down. I say that because, it is a known fact, that there is someone that we focus on more than ourselves. In my case, it was all about my grandchildren, my children, my marriage, and how I would pay my bills. All the while I had my eyes on those things, I had forgotten me, and little by little my life was falling apart.

It was choking me out and I didn't even know it! And to be honest, I was so focused on them, and and the things that were going on around me, I hadn't even realized that I was neglecting myself. I gave my everything to them and I was left with nothing. One day I fell, and it took me a long time to get up. I was asking the ones that were around me to bring me a glass of water only for them to not hear me. In my down times, my cries were unheard by the ones that I gave my up time to. But God!!!

Jesus said, "My child, I got you. I gave you legs to move, why are you not using them? Go get your own water. There is no need for you to be hungry because I am your bread, and I will provide for your other food. But you've got to use those legs that I blessed you with to prepare your food. Why are you breaking yourself down trying to work not one job, but two jobs? You are trying to make sure everyone get their wants, I provide for you all of your needs, but you are using your blessings to take care of them."

I Jackie, had to take a real close look in the mirror, but I still couldn't see in me what Jesus sees in me. What I saw in the mirror, was hurt, pain, anger, bitterness, all that I had lost and that I was still losing. I had written two books and started on another until, I had lost my will to write. There was so much I wanted to say in my book, but my mind, heart and hands had gone on strike. At first, I couldn't figure out what was going on with me and then Jesus said,

"My child you looked away, you took on burdens that were not meant for you to carry. You were so busy fixing it for everyone else, you forgot to laugh, you forgot to enjoy your blessings, you forgot about Jackie. If you are not in your right mind you can't take care of yourself or no one else around you."

I had to take my eyes off my grandchildren, off my children, and off my problems, because sometimes we could be holding onto some stuff, that God has been trying to move out of our lives. While praying one night, pouring my heart out to God, He said,

"The door is open by faith, I just need you to make up your mind to just walk through it and carry my burdens for they are light. Lay down your cross and follow me." Once I made that decision, my life took on a new meaning, a new purpose. Things begin to crash around me. I was so focused on JESUS to work things out for me, that I didn't even see the crash. Things begin to fall in place for me instead of on top of me. Doors started opening and I was determined that I was going to walk on toward the goal that had been set for me and there's no turning back. My burdens are lighter, my mind is renewed, and my heart belongs to Jesus. When others want to walk away from you, let them go. Because you know in your heart, you've given all you had to give. Love will win in the end because God is Love.

5

Love Broke

My love has been bruised for a long time. You hear people say that love doesn't supposed to hurt but I am here to tell you that's a lie. Love does hurt. Love will bring the strongest person down. Love hurts. It even hurts to care sometimes.

The older I get, the more I realize that I also need love. I have never doubted God's love for me and I always say as long as I've got God's don't need anything else. But HE created me with a great and love broke me. I was always busy loving everyone else and I had forgotten that I needed love too. I need a kind voice, a gentle hug, or just to hear someone say, "Jackie, I love you, or just a smile. Loving others and having them not love you back really does hurt.

I was so busy loving others, and being hurt that I let love pass me by.
God was sending others to love me and I was so hurt and so blind that I let my love pass me by.
When I realized that I needed love also, it opened my eyes. I know I will neve stop loving others but I will also make time to love myself. Because if I'm not loving me, there's no way I can love others the way I'm supposed to.

Only the love of God is enough. Once we really accept the fact that God really loves us, our life will take on a new meaning.

It is only through divine wisdom that we can ever understand what it means to truly be loved by God.

There is no human love that could ever compare to God's love. We can.

't

Even love our children the way that God loves us. All we can do is pray for the fullness of God to help us understand John 3:16. God have His Son for us. Sometimes God will allow us to catch a glimpse of what this scripture really mean for those who accept His Son for just a moment it is as if He unveils the true power of His Love and we are struck blind by it, then it's gone, our flesh is incapable of handling the fullness of God for any length of time. So we go from Glory to Glory and that sustains is until the day that everlasting is fully and finally revealed. That is why love broke me, because I didn't understand it.

1 John 4:18, there is no fear in prefect love, but perfect love casteth out fear: Jesus is love and we should not fear in following Him. We should want to encourage others to come and go with us.

We should also want others to come and get to know God so they can feel the same love as we do.

That is the reason for me writing, and sharing with others because there's something for us all to learn from each other. I want to encourage someone that accepting Jesus will be the best decided that they could ever make.

I'm not saying that everything will fall into place at one because the struggle is real. But isn't it good to know we have a God as our Father, who is about to provide for us? This is why we should not worry when troubling situations come against us.

Think of the things that you have already dealt with, they

are a part of your past now, all because God loved you enough to deliver you. This alone should show you that there is a God and He loves you. He can and He will handle your situation no matter what it might be. Your only focus shroff should be trusting Him and nothing else. With God handling things for us we should be thanking Him that we can now move freely. With God's love, comes deliverance, power, joy, love, peace, wisdom, understanding and renewed grace and mercy everyday Galatians 5:22-23.

6

A Wake Up Call

There are so many things that I have done in my life that I consider right. But the best thing I've ever done, was to open the door to my heart and invite Jesus to come in and be the head of my life and my heart.

I do not consider myself to be perfect, But I am striving to do what Jesus wants me to do. I saw more in myself than I should have, my peace was being tested, day after day. My joy slowly started slipping away. I found myself in spiritual warfare that was caused by me, because I continued to ignore my wake up call. Everyday I was allowed to wake up to new grace and new mercy but because of the things I was facing in life, I took my eyes off the ONE who woke me up. I had to realize that the same God I poured my heart out to and asked Him to be head over my life is the same God who showed me that He would make me the head and not the tail. And that I would be above and not beneath. But He said this is if I hearken to His commandments.

Wake up call: Why have I got my eyes on the problem and not the Problem Solver?
God said, "Do not be afraid or discouraged. I will personally go

ahead of you and I will be with you and I will neither fail nor abandon you.
Who in their right mind would want to live a life without God?

Wake up call: The only things in life that has control over us are the things that we give in to. God has allowed us to come a long ways and for me, that is too far to turn around now.
The devil tried to pull me down, he's crafty and will use anyone and anything against you. But God commands us to not be afraid and not to get discouraged. The battle is not ours, but His.
Life is full of surprises some good and some that will try to destroy you. Not every day is going to be what you expect but remember in your weakness God is strong. When you feel like giving up remind yourself to keep going and remain focused on God, the One who goes before you. There has been so many things that have made me want to turn back, but God is faithful to do all that he has said He would do and I will not turn back and I pray that you don't either.

There were things I wanted to do, and places I wanted to go. I soon found out that these things were not for me and it wasn't time to go to those places yet. God had other plans for me.
Philippians 2:13, For it is God which worketh in us both to will and to do of His good pleasure. Philippians 2:16 we've got to hold forth the word of life that we may move on and rejoice in the day of Christ that we have not run in vane neither labored in vane. Only the things of Christ will last.
In order to move on, and not look back, we have got to worship God in Spirit and rejoice in Christ Jesus no matter how things will or may look at the moment. We have got to keep our eyes on Jesus and not ourselves. In order for us to not look back with the world

eyes we have to count our gain as loss for Christ Philippians 3:7. We have to be found in Him not having our own righteousness but that which through the faith of Christ the righteousness which is of God by faith to move on. Philippians 3:9. We have to forget those things which are behind us, we have to press toward the mark of the prize of the high calling of God in Christ Jesus, Philippians 3:13-14.

7

The Past

The Past-something from a second or a minute ago is your past. There are a lot of people that you will come across in your lifetime that do not want to see you succeed in life and they have nothing better than to try and bring up your past, like they don't have one of their own.

We all have a past and we all have a future, We also have a choice whether we live in our past or move on toward our future and the goal that God has set for us.

Philippians 1:6 tells us that we can be confident that He (Jesus) which hath begun a good work in us will perform it until He comes again. Once you accept Jesus as your Lord and Savior our life that we live become a part or our past.

Philippians 1:21 for us to live is Christ and to die is gain. When we made the decision to choose Christ, we made the decision to die to our old self.

We can declare that we are not past, we are future. We have been bought with a price and nothing can change that. We can move forward and not look back because there is not one thing that we can go back and change but the good news is that Jesus has redeemed us, so our past has no control over our future.

Hallelujah, Hallelujah! Our name is not our past but redeemed. Do not let what was in your past define who you are. We can move on with confidence and not look back.

Knowing that our beloved Father knows the plans He has for our life, Jeremiah 29.11. God says, For I know the plans I have for you plans to prosper you and not to harm you, plans to give you hope and a future.

There is going to be a time while on this journey, FEAR is going to knock on your door but all you have to do is let FAITH answer. Faith is freedom. It is trusting God and believing that He and only He can do the impossible. God says, "Take no thoughts of tomorrow and be anxious for nothing, Do not be afraid to move forward because you can overcome fear by reading and believing God's word and strengthen your relationship with Him and not the world.
God is working with us, in us and through us and His perfect love will drive our fear.
Let Go and Let God! Move on toward the goals God has for you. Move forward and don't look back. Don't let nothing or nobody stop you from moving forward and being the best that you can be. Pray and ask God to send someone that will lift you up and encourage you to move on.
Psalm 37
3. Trust in the Lord and do good
4. Delight yourself in the Lord
5. Commit your ways to the Lord and trust in Him.

Don't take anger, bitterness or anything else not of God with you moving forward.
11. The meek shall inherit the earth and shall delight themselves in the abundance of peace.
Move forward with your head held high.
23. The steps of a good man are ordered by the Lord.
Don't be afraid to leave your past.
God says to you: He is near, He is fighting your battles, He created you, you are His treasure, and He loves you.

8

Going Forward

We have seen the mighty power of God working in so many people lives and how He has helped them to overcome so many battles in their lives. And that same power of God that worked then, still works now and it is able to save us.

Going forward we have to have a made up mind to know that God is God and there is no other God that can truly save us. God is still in the business of helping us to overcome whatever we may face in the days, months and years ahead of us. All we have to do is spend one second, one minute, one hour accepting His love, guidance, and directions from His word. Our challenges may be bigger than us, but they will never bigger than God. So let's go forward knowing that weeping may endure for a night but joy really does come in the morning, Psalm 30:5.

Every day that God allow us to see is another day to move a little further and to become stronger in our relationship with Him. On our own, we can do nothing right. In Matthew 19:26, Jesus said, "with man this is impossible, but with God all things are possible. I am just in awe when I think about the mess that I made in my life, I know I don't deserve to be alive. The path that I was on was leading me straight to death. I was lost, I was walking around in despair, I was eating bitterness, keeping company with envy, self-pity and anger. I was mad at the world but in true reality it was all me. I was looking for love in all the wrong places. I was running and didn't even know what I was running from. I had so many dark days and teary nights. I was going to church but I was not hearing what the preacher was saying. I only thought about how deep I was falling with no way up. But then I heard a voice, and it said to me,

"Open up and let me in. Behold I stand at the door and knock. If anyone hears my voice open the door and I will come in to hm and sup with him and he with me," Revelation 3:20. The Bible dictionary meaning for the word, "sup" is to dine, to make a meal. Once I opened the door to my heart and let Jesus in, my life has never been the same.

I asked the Lord to deliver me, to walk with me, and talk with me. I asked God to change my soul, my heart, and my mind. I started living on faith and not feelings. I chose to live the life that God allowed me to start over with. I have no regret but I choose to leave the past where it belongs, in the past.

BE AN OVER-COMER

There has been some very painful moments in my life that have caused me to make some changes. They made me stronger, smarter, and more kind. But I will never let it make me become someone that I am not. I have cried, screamed and had many sleepless nights. But now, I have straightened up my crown and started moving again.

Thank You Jesus that my pain became a praise! God has shown me that He's going to restore everything the devil tried to take from me.

My days of pain are over!
My days of sorrow are over!

My days of begging are over!
My days of problems are over!
My days of struggling are over!
My days of complaints are over!
My days of devastation are over!
My days and nights of tears are over!
In the Mighty Name of Jesus they are over!

I claim victory over everything that tried to destroy me. I am so confident in God's plans for my life, I will not get upset any more when things don't go my way. I am stepping into my new! It's a new me! I am getting ready to walk into my promise. I am getting ready to take back everything that was taken from me! God is about to make my life unrecognizable. I believe and I receive it! Lord what is my new name? What is my spiritual name that you have given me?

Lord though you slay me, I still will trust You. Devil flee from me, because I am the head and not the tail. I am above and not beneath. I am more than a conqueror. I am blessed in the city. I am blessed in the field. I am blessed in my uprising and blessed in my down-setting. No matter where I go, I am blessed! Father thank You that this is my season, and that everything I speak, it is so. Everything I desire, it is so. Father thank You that our finances are blessed, our marriages are blessed, our children are blessed and it is so! Thank You Father that my dreams will be blessed, it is so.

Thank You Father that I can walk in total victory!

God thinks of me everyday, Psalm 68:16
Every hour God looks after me 2 Thessalonians 3:3
Every minute, God cares for me 1 Peter 5:7
Because every second He loves me.

Pray and invite the Holy Spirit to lead and guide you and to help you know the will of God so you can move on and live the life that God has for you to live.

9

Me and My Big Mouth

Have you ever opened your mouth and words just started pouring out of it, and then later on you think back on some of the stuff you said and just start crying or laughing non stop? There is power in the tongue, James 3:5. Words can build someone up or tear them down. Words can stir up anger or they can calm the soul. In James 3:8, it says that no man can tame the tongue. There are some things that we say out of our mouth that we wish we could take back but once they are out we cannot pull them back in.

I know that I have a big mouth and I don't mind speaking what's on my mind. But I want only the things to come out of my mouth that will build others up and glorify God. I am learning that sometimes it's better to remain silent and just smile.

I have used my mouth as the world has wanted me to use it, saying things that often hurt others not because I wasn't speaking what was real and true but because of how I was saying it.

Now I just want to encourage someone to know that there's nothing wrong with falling down as long as you don't stay down.

During my down times, were when I learned what to say and how to say it. Being down allowed me time with God to learn how to speak. Now I want to use my big mouth to please and bring glory to God by saying things to bring others up. There are some things that I have spoken out of my mouth that I can't take back and would not take them back even if I could. And then there are some things that I have said that I wish with my whole heart that I could take back.

1 Corinthians 13:11, says When I was a child, I didn't know better and I didn't think about the words I spoke or the way I spoke them but now I know better and I will do better. James 3:5 says the tongue is a small part of the body but it is very dangerous.

Proverbs 12:18, the tongue has life and death and power and those who love it will eat its fruit.

Proverbs 18:21, the tongue has the power of life and death. It it time for us to start thinking about what we say. A gentle tongue is a tree of life, but the perverseness in it breaks the spirit.

1 Corinthians 13:11 When I was a child I spoke like a child, I thought like a child I reasoned like a child. When I became an adult I no longer used childish ways.

Proverbs 18:21 The tongue has the power of life and death. Be careful how you speak your words because they can speak life or death, they can build up or tear down.

Proverbs 12:18 Death and life are in the power of the tongue and those who love it will eat its fruit.

James 3:5 the tongue is a small part of the body, but it makes great boasts. Words are formidable. They can build up and tear down. They can stir up anger and they can soothe the soul.

Choose your words to bring glory and honor to God.

10

Speak Over Your Life

There are times that we need to think about what we are saying to ourselves. Our thoughts feed our faith and it also feeds our fear. Stop talking negative about your situation no matter how it looks. Remember God has a plan, Jeremiah 29:11 says, For I know the thoughts that I think towards you, saith the Lord, thoughts of peace and not of evil, to give you an expected end.

If you want a change renew your thoughts, Ephesians 2:20 says, I am crucified with Christ: nevertheless I live, yet not I but Christ liveth in me and I am living by faith. Tell yourself, "I have control over this because God said in Deuteronomy 28:13, He will make me the head and not the tail. I am above and not beneath. We only have to hearken to His word, obey and observe and do them.

Tell yourself,
I am who God made me. I am blessed, I am debt-free, I am healed, set-free and delivered. My children are blessed, everyone connected to me is blessed.

Tell yourself,
Psalm 23:4, Yea though I walk through the valley of the shadow of death, I will fear no evil for I know God is with me.

And I know Psalm 23, Surely goodness and mercy shall follow me all the days of my life and I will dwell in the house of the Lord forever. So to get to me, you have to pass through my Father who stands at the door.

Please know that when you speak, you can cause the earth to move in the mighty power of God.

Speak to the chains that have you bound. Chains in my life, be broken in the mighty name of Jesus.

Tell yourself,

that you are going to keep on praising God and He will set you free.

Psalm 23:5, says God will prepare a table for you in the presence of your enemies. God will take the things that are tearing us down to build us up.

Tell yourself,

You are loved by an Amazing God. Once you start speaking life you will start living life. Once you start speaking peace, peace will overtake you.

There is power in the tongue. Power of life and death. So speak life and live.

Tell yourself,

I am debt-free, I am successful, I am healed, set-free and delivered. My children are saved, they are obedient and they are positive history makers. My cup is running over today, tomorrow and for the rest of my sanctified life. My neighborhood is blessed. My church is in the overflow in every way.

My mouth is something serious cause when I speak the earth moves in the mighty name of God.

We have to learn to break the chains on ourselves before we try to break them off our situation. In all and any situation we have to keep on praising God and He will set us free. God will prepare our table in front of our enemies.

Tell yourself,
that you have a God in your life that is able to help you withstand any challenges that comes your way. Let your light shine so others will see it and want to move forward toward the goal God has set for them.

11

A Better Me

As I sit and watch things fall around me and in my life, I saw things get turned upside down, nothing was working for me. Then I realized that I had taken my eyes off God and was looking at the problems. I realized in order for there to be a better me, I had to have a shift in my life. It was time for me to make some decisions that would determine my destiny. There is so much we take for granted in life. I once heard it said that we can be an ordinary thinker. I want to see changes in my life, so I can choose to become a disrupted thinker. I chose to leave my comfort zone and walk by faith to the unknown.

In order for me to become a better me, I had to disrupt my way of thinking and my life as I knew it to be. I wanted to be on the knowing end of knowing that God can and He is able to take care of me. I had to learn to stand under the peace of all understanding. I choose God's peace and I will not let life crush me. While my marriage was falling apart, death was all around me, kids getting out of control and my health was failing. I found out that you can't have a changed life without disruption but you don't have to let the disruption take over your life. For a long time, I let the disruption take over my life not wanting to come out of my comfort zone, not wanting to try anything new but as started to look at my life, I decided it was time to move forward and not look back.

I had to learn to be content with everything and I had to learn to be content with nothing.

Philippians 4:11-13, I had to learn that whatsoever state I was in to be content. I had to be content knowing that God was mine and I am His and that He is with me and without Him I am nothing. With Him I can do all things because He is my strength. I had to encourage myself that the same God that I tell others about is the same God that will also take care of me.

When things go wrong in your life as they sometimes will, you can trust God to do just what He said He would do. Numbers 23:19, God is not a man that he should lie, neither the Son of Man that He should repent. If He say He will do it, then we can count it done. We can be a better us, because God said it in His word. So I am not just staying where I am. I want the life God said I could have.

At one time, I thought I had it going on with the life I was living. I was always trying to change others to get them to see the things I was seeing. I had to realize that what I was seeing was the things God had only for my eyes and that He was working on me. Work it Lord! You are the Potter and I am the clay, make me into what You want me to be.

Be a better you and let God have total control for His Glory. Don't stress over what you can't control just take control over what you can.

12

The Fight of My Life

Closing this chapter of my life, has really took a toll on me mentally, physically and spiritually. After twelve years of marriage, my husband decided that he would just walk out. I had so many mixed emotions. I was lost, then found. I was blinded by this and then I started to see. I was speechless, but then became full of words. I was sad but I received joy. I was lonely, but not alone.

I fought a thousand fights within myself but I knew giving up was not an option. I cried a thousand tears, but, I continued to smile through it all. I was broken, betrayed, abandoned and rejected but, I STILL HELD MY HEAD UP AND WALKED PROUD.

When I love, I love hard, because I know that's what God wants me to do. On my own, I was nothing but I humbled myself and decided to allow God to use me for His glory. The road I was on, was not easy to travel but worth traveling. That road has gotten me to where I am now. There was no understanding but God helped me to understand so much. God did not remove my situation, but He used it to show me the power of prayer and the importance of seeking His guidance. God is teaching me about the importance of discernment and wisdom in my choices.

God is using this experience to help me better understand His love and His grace. God is in control and He will guide me through this journey even if it was very difficult to understand. Until the end of my time, I will remain faithful to God who can and will restore everything I've lost.

Sometimes, you have to hurt and keep on going because life does not stop. Though He slay me, I will still trust Him. He has shown me this was not the end but the beginning. With all the hurt and pain from my marriage, my children, my so-called friends and my health failing, out of everything coming against me, God showed me that He was the Master to call on. He was the answer to all of my problems, all of my pain. He showed my that any and everything is possible to them that believe. Prayer is the answer.

Dear Lord

As I enter into a new day, I turn to You in prayer. I acknowledge that this entire day is a precious gift from You filled with countless opportunities and blessings. In this moment, I seek your presence and guidance. I am grateful for the gift of this day and all the blessings it holds. Father help me approach it with a heart full of gratitude. Grant me the wisdom to discern Your will and the courage to follow it whole-heartedly. Father may my thoughts, words and actions align with Your divine purpose throughout this day's journey. I surrender my plans and desires to You. I trust in Your infinite wisdom and ask for Your guidance in all that I do. Lead me on the path of righteousness and reveal your divine plans for my life and protect me from many challenges, temptations, or negativity that may come my way. Fill me with Your strength Lord, so I can be the person You want me to be and do the things You want me to do in Jesus Name Amen.

Now it is time to grow. I regret nothing that has happened in my life, even if my past was full of hurt, I still can look back and smile because it made me the woman that I am today. VICTORY is mine and yours! I Won! The pain didn't make me bitter but it made me better. I won! I fell but I got back up. I won! I could have let hate consume me but I chose to love instead. I won! The devil thought he had me but Jesus reached down and grabbed me. It is growth when you can move forward no longer thinking about how things could be but knowing God and the power of prayer.

Don't let what you see make you forget what God has said. Take life day by day and be grateful for the little things. Let go and Let God! Walk On!

No Turning Back!

GIVING THANKS TO GOD

GIVING THANKS TO GOD NO MATTER WHAT'S GOING ON

God is saying, Sometimes you have to go through the worst to get to the best. God is saying I am with you and that alone, is enough to give thanks to God! Because one day you will be able to look and say I made it all because of God.

When you go to God and ask for anything you must believe that He's going to give it to you! Give Him thanks and praise Him like you have already received it.

He is a Rewarder of those who diligently seek Him. God is our Bread, when we are hungry, O taste and see the goodness of the Lord Psalm 34:8. And in your dark time God is the light, 1 John 1:5.

www.ingramcontent.com/pod-product-compliance
Lightning Source LLC
Chambersburg PA
CBHW050046080526
44586CB00014B/1489